photo**word**book

Seasons

Sue Barraclough

WAYLAND

First published in 2007 by Wayland

Copyright © Wayland 2007

Wayland
338 Euston Road
London NW1 3BH

Wayland Australia
Level 17/207 Kent Street
Sydney, NSW 2000

Design: Natascha Frensch
Typography: Natascha Frensch
Read Regular (European Community Design Registration 2003)
Read Regular and Read Xheavy copyright © Natascha Frensch 2001-2006

Editor: Joyce Bentley
Picture research: Sue Barraclough

ISBN 978 0 7502 5149 5

Printed in China

Wayland is a division of Hachette Children's Books, an Hachette Livre UK Company.

Acknowledgements: Cover © image100/Corbis; p 1,12 & 22 © Comstock/Corbis; pp 2-3 © Dietrich Rose/
zefa/Corbis; pp 4-5 Kathy Collins/Photographer's Choice/Getty; pp 6-7 & 22 © Robert Llewellyn/zefa/Corbis;
pp 8-9 © image100/Corbis; p 11 & 22 © Bloomimage/Corbis; p13 & 22 Anne Ackerman/Taxi/Getty; p15
Ian Boddy, Science Photo Library; p16 Simon Wilkinson/Iconica/Getty; p17 Superstudio/Taxi/Getty; pp 16-17
© Richard Hamilton Smith/Corbis; pp 20-21 © Craig Tuttle/Corbis

2

Contents

3

season

A **season** is a time of year.

spring

summer

4

Each season has different weather.

autumn

winter

5

spring

Spring is a season.

New green leaves and flowers grow.

7

summer

Summer is a season.

We play outside in warm weather.

sky

The **sky** is blue in summer.

Butterflies fly from flower
to flower.

autumn

Autumn is a season.

Some leaves change colour.

windy

Autumn is **windy.**

Windy weather is good for flying a kite.

13

leaves

In autumn, **leaves** fall.

This girl plays in the **leaves**.

winter

Winter is a season.

Many trees have no leaves.

cold

Winter is **cold**.

We wear warm clothes in winter.

snow

In winter, it can **snow**.

Playing in the snow is fun!

rainbow

We see **rainbows** in all seasons.

Sunshine and rain make a **rainbow** of many colours.

Picture quiz

Can you find these things in the book?

kite

flowers

butterfly

leaves

What pages are they on?

Index quiz

The index is on page 24.
Use the index and pictures
to answer these questions.

1. Which pages show **snow**?
   How many sledges can you count?

2. Which pages show summer is **warm**?
   How many children are playing?

3. Which pages show a **rainbow**?
   What two things make a rainbow?

4. Which page shows winter is **cold**?
   How many woolly hats can you see?

Index

Answers

Picture quiz: The kite is on page 13. The flowers are on page 7. The butterfly is on page 11. The leaves are on page 12.
Index quiz: 1. Page 18-19, three; 2. Page 9-10, three; 3. Page 20-21, sun and rain; 4. Page 17, one.